This book belongs to

Phone Number

E-mail

Made in United States
Troutdale, OR
12/10/2025

43483929R00062